36,000 Days
of
Japanese Music

The Culture of Japan Through A Look At Its Music

KOH-ICHI HATTORI

PacificVision BOOKS

The original manuscript was edited by
    The Writing Team, Hazel Richmond Dawkins, Pennsylvania.
Cover design, some of the art, and typography by
    Pacific Vision, Kyo Takahashi, Michigan.
Photographs assembled by the author with the permission of
    copyright holders.

Library of Congress Catalog Card Number: 96-69976
Hattori, Koh-ichi
36,000 Days of Japanese Music.
        Includes index.
1. Japan — Music History — Music Education — 1860 ~
2. Music — Japan — History — Education — 1860 ~
Printed and published in the United States of America.

ISBN 0-9653642-0-8
First Edition

Contents

Preface

During the last several decades, as I have traveled outside Japan and had the experience of giving numerous concerts and lectures, I have discovered that most people have limited information about modern Japan and its culture.

They may know the name of Mount Fuji or have tried *sukiyaki* (which actually is not authentic Japanese cuisine, as I note later). Perhaps they know about the traditional stage show, *kabuki,* which is now really special to the average Japanese, who may not even actually see kabuki during his or her entire life. They know of and even own Japanese cars named Toyota or Honda and television sets produced by Sony or Panasonic. Yet they do not know about the people who developed these products, and they do not know about the culture of Japan. Indeed, their basic understanding about my country may be that it is a place where good products are made and sold at competitive prices.

It is my belief that the twenty-first century is the century when we all need to try to unify, to make our world one family. The essence of mutual understanding comes more readily when other cultural backgrounds are known. When we learn about the culture of a country, we acquire clues to understanding the people and the place. It is also true that learning about the musical life of Japan is a connection to understanding the minds of the people who make good automobiles.

Of the myriad comments and analysis by Westerners about Japan, its culture and its music, perhaps some of the most telling are to be found in *Windows for the Crown Prince*, the book by the American Quaker chosen to tutor the heir to Japan's monarchy (now Emperor Akihito) after World War II. In this book, author Elizabeth Gray Vining described a performance arranged for her at a Shinto shrine. "The musicians who wore ancient costumes of green, played the weirdest music I had ever heard, on instruments that I had never before seen. ... Sometimes the music made me think of a saxophone, sometimes of the Scotch bagpipes, sometimes of Ravel's *Bolero*, though it was none of these. It was primitive and also extremely sophisticated. None of the discords was unintended and the effect on the raw nerves was entirely calculated."

Whether we scrutinize the intangibles — the music — or the tangibles — the materials manufactured — we learn slowly and surely about others. Edwin O. Reischauer, United States Ambassador to Japan from 1961~66, was confident that Japan could contribute significantly to the future, to a global community of the new century. In *The Japanese*, he suggested that as a great and wealthy country that has "renounced war and maintains only a very modest Self-Defense Force, Japan may help all nations find their way past the crushing burden of military rivalries to a more peaceful and prosperous age."

Surely, we ask, the essence of mutual understanding comes more readily when other cultural backgrounds are known. It is my belief that the twenty-first century is the century when we all need to try to unify, to make our world one family.

Grateful acknowledgment is due to Tokyo Kasei University and its Graduate School Professorship Committee, headed by Professor Akimichi Yamanouchi, for the 1995 grant which made it possible for me to finish this work.

I am indebted to Tad Fujimatsu of Japan Airlines for the wealth of advice he has shared with me. His perception of the international experience is profound and has been particularly meaningful to me.

Acknowledgment also goes to the staff at the Harvard University Library Archives and the Bridgewater State College Library for their ever-helpful support with the research necessary to complete this book.

Thanks go to Hazel Richmond Dawkins, Managing Editor of the Writing Team, who has worked carefully with me on this book. The splendid collaboration of Kyo Takahashi of Pacific Vision, a long-time friend of mine, for the design and publication — he even drew some of the illustrations — is deeply appreciated.

Koh-ichi Hattori
Kamakura, Japan
Fall, 1996

Introduction

The cultural behavior of the Japanese and the lifestyle of contemporary Japan are of considerable interest to many. Some may consider that Japan is one of the world's leading automobile manufacturers, for we see many Japanese cars in countries outside Japan. Unfortunately, sales of Japanese cars in some Western countries have created international trade friction simply because such sales are so strong.

How clearly I recall the situation of the automobile industry in Japan fifty years ago, immediately after World War II. Those were the days when we could hardly make automobiles, other than poor quality trucks and buses. Very few people in the country could afford to own a private car. In fact, we actually had to use U.S. military trucks as city buses — these massive vehicles rolled down the Ginza, Tokyo's central avenue, the equivalent of London's Bond Street or Fifth Avenue in New York. What a tremendous change Japan has made since then!

That was an era when Japan was faced with a serious food short-age. Yet all we really wanted to do was listen to beautiful music, mainly Western classics — Beethoven, Mozart and the works of Chopin. Barely one month after the end of the war (August 15, 1945), NHK (the National Broadcasting Corporation) Symphony Orchestra — which at that time was the only symphony in existence — held a concert at Hibiya Public Hall, the one hall that had some-how survived the devastating American Boeing B-29 bomber air raids which had reduced downtown Tokyo to ashes. The music-loving people formed a long line to buy tickets. Earnestly, they lis-tened to Beethoven's *Symphony No. 3* in spite of their nearly empty stomachs. Evidently, they had been thirsty for Western music even as they endured those air raids.

In January 1946, five months after the end of World War II, Tokyo was enjoying Verdi's opera *La Traviata*. This was the favorite opera in Japan and had been played many times before the war; the first grand performance took place in Tokyo in 1930. After enjoy-ing the beautiful stage scenes of the sumptuous mid-nineteenth century salon, the Japanese people returned to live in the shabby huts they had improvised among the ruins of their homes. Their entrance tickets had cost as much as they would normally spend for meals for many days, which shows the considerable respect of the Japanese for Western classical music and culture.

Traditional Japanese music had not been revived by that time. As for popular music, American jazz (which had been received with widespread enthusiasm before the war) was as pervasive as the American Occupation of Japan and was a considerable influence on Japanese popular tunes.

Karaoke — where one sings along with a recorded tape as an accompaniment — is an interesting Japanese invention. Karaoke rapidly became popular in Japan over the last twenty years, a trend which spread quickly. Karaoke is now available and thoroughly enjoyed in many countries. Easy and gratifying, it is a combination of electronic techniques and the natural desire to sing and be accompanied by an orchestra. Interestingly enough, part of the benefit to the individual who performs in this way comes from exercising pitch control and from the side effects of the artificial reverbration added to the singing voice. Karaoke is an illustration of the typical character of Japan's people and culture.

It is my hope that as I introduce the musical life and the state of music in Japan, readers will also learn something of the subtleties of our culture. Perhaps this book will help to explain some of the ways we Japanese have of thinking. It is quite rare that a nation truly enjoys and cultivates the music of a culture ethnically foreign to them the way that Japan does. Indeed, the number in the title *36,000 Days* refers to a century of musical life in Japan. We are all agreed that the culture of Japan is totally different from that of Western nations. Historically and ethnically, Japanese culture is derived from China. We have borrowed Chinese characters to write Japanese and even the phonetic syllabary *kana* is composed in some small part of Chinese characters. Japanese customs and manners are historically related to China.

No one would deny that Japan is an Oriental country. Yet daily life is patterned on what are virtually Western ways. Consider eating habits: bread and butter at breakfast, spaghetti napolitan at lunch and beef for the biggest meal of the day. Such meal combinations are quite common for Japanese families. On the other hand, the most popular Japanese foods outside Japan, *sushi* or

A popular Japanese lunch at a family restaurant: hamburger steak, pickles, white rice and *miso* soup, each in their own bowl.

sukiyaki, nowadays are rather special and not everyday dishes for Japanese families.

The two disparate situations I have discussed, one concerning the fine arts, the other, the quality of living, were part of the fabric of life in Japan directly after World War II. Indeed, I would like to say that the automobile and do-re-mi-fa music (based on commonly used scales in Western music, such as major or Ionian mode) are not Japanese in origin at all. The truth is that we Japanese have a tendency to become interested in new concepts, activities and ideas and absorb them quickly. We are then innovative with them. Frequently we even embrace such ideas by adopting them into our culture. Perhaps this is why Edwin Reischauer wrote that: "The river of history flows fast in Japan, and each bend reveals the country in a new light."

The Meiji Restoration
(Meiji Ishin)

Japan's association with Western culture is relatively recent and was initiated some hundred years ago during the period of *Meiji Ishin,* or the Meiji Restoration, approximately 1867~1872. That was the era, under the reign of the Meiji Emperor (1868~1912), when Japan turned from the feudal to the modern age. Japanese feudal rulers, the Tokugawa government (the so-called Shogun government), followed a policy of national isolationism from 1639~ 1853. Neither cultural exchange nor the entry of Western culture was permitted in those years.

The growing awareness among the Japanese of the West prompted the Meiji government to study the ideas and cultures of the Western hemisphere, specifically those with advanced technologies. Intelligent Japanese acknowledged that Japan was far behind the Western world and that there was much to be learned from the West.

"Catch up with them, learn from them, pass them" *(oi-tsuke, mana-be, oi-kose)* was the slogan of the leaders of Japan. The population was so receptive to outside influences during the Meiji period that a steady stream of Western products and customs poured in — from hair styles to clothes, locomotives and telegraphs. Railroads were built to the north and the south for steam trains. The nation's constitution was based on that of Germany while the educational system was adopted from the French. The Japanese even began to eat the flesh of four-footed animals publicly. Called *gyu-nabe,* the equivalent of sukiyaki, this was something which up till then had been prohibited by Buddhism.

In what was, socially, a relatively short time (approximately one decade), the circumstances in Japan had changed tremendously. It is appropriate to say that the Meiji era was the locomotive that pulled Japan into modern times.

The Enjoyment of Music
in Japan Today

The intent of this book is to share with you how music is enjoyed in Japan today. In turn, this is a key to learning about the country and its culture. We Japanese are really fond of do-re-mi-fa music, which was introduced to Japan a mere one hundred years ago.

As mentioned, the Meiji government established a new educational system based on that of the French. However, the new system in Japan included music as a subject at the elementary school level, although music as a subject was not included in the French system. America was the first to include music in the elementary curriculum in the 1830s in the Boston area. Japanese educators followed the American initiative even though they had to include the subject in an educational framework that was essentially French. This type of innovation shows the flexibility of the Japanese to make significant adaptations that will have long-term benefits.

Now for some pictures of the unique musical life in Japan and its background, which will help deepen understanding of my country.

Do-Re-Mi-Fa Country

The most popular and widespread type of music in today's Japan is Western music. The Japanese enjoyment of music centers around the Western sound. Even our folk songs are accompanied by Western musical instruments such as the guitar, saxophone and piano. American-style jazz bands are frequently used as accompaniments at traditional folk music concerts. When you ask children what instruments they have at home, almost all will answer either piano, guitar or electronic organ — the latter is now the trend unless the youngster is the daughter of a traditional musician who plays the *koto*, the most popular traditional instrument.

Generally speaking, Japan is the country of do-re-mi-fa music. The importance of the traditional musical arts and how they are preserved or integrated into contemporary Japanese music is quite significant and is contained in separate chapters. Here I would simply like to describe both what is going on musically in our society and Japan's musical perspective today.

Mrs.Kimiko Namura playing the traditional koto.

Orchestras and Operas

In Japan, we have some twenty-four professional symphony orchestras. In my personal judgment, one-third of these orchestras can be ranked as international in class. All of the orchestras have invited famous conductors such as Herbert von Karajan, Leonard Bernstein and Claudio Abbado to their podiums as well as many distinguished soloists. The truth is, every world virtuoso willingly comes to Japan and

Maestro Hiroyuki Iwaki, permanent conductor of the NHK Symphony Orchestra.

presents concerts in cooperation with these orchestras.

The Tokyo metropolitan area has nine such groups:
- NHK Symphony Orchestra was founded in 1926 and is the oldest existing orchestra in the nation;
- Tokyo Philharmonic Orchestra;
- Tokyo Symphonic Orchestra;
- Shin-Nihon Philharmonic;
- Tokyo Metropolitan Symphony Orchestra;
- Nihon Philharmonic Symphony Orchestra;
- Yomiuri Nihon Symphony Orchestra;
- Tokyo City Philharmonic Orchestra;
- Shinsei Nihon Symphony Orchestra.

NHK Symphony Orchestra.

When was European opera first performed in Japan? The date was August 1903, at the Tokyo National Music College. It was Gluck's *Orfeo ed Euridice*. The singers were all students at the college and they were directed by Professor Noel Perry of France. The only accompaniment was Professor Raphael Koeber (1848~1923) on the piano (at this point, an orchestra had not yet been organized at the college and Professor Koeber, a fine pianist, actually lectured on German philosophy at Tokyo University but enjoyed this extracurricular activity).

Grand opera performed by an all-Japanese cast of musicians had to wait until February 1930, when Verdi's *La Traviata* was presented. It was directed by the distinguished musician Kohsaku Yamada. Before that, small European opera traveling companies visited Japan with shows such as *Boccacio* and *Heaven and Hell*. Japanese performers had also presented parts of grand operas.

In the first decade of the 1900s, many of the melodies from European operettas became quite popular in Japan. Cheap reproductions would appear overnight in Asakusa, the theatrical section of downtown Tokyo. However, for all intents and purposes, the first true presentation of opera was that original performance of *La Traviata* in 1930 at Kabuki-za (the special theater for kabuki plays).

In 1934, the first Japanese opera company, the Fujiwara Opera, resumed production and became quite well established through the performance of Puccini's *La Boheme* at the Hibiya Hall in Tokyo.

Yasuko Hayashi as Tosca and
Taro Ichihara as Cavaradossi
— Fujiwara Opera 1995 —

Today, Japan has two major opera companies, the Fujiwara Opera and the Nikikai Opera. Both regularly present all the standard numbers as well as contemporary works. In recent years, each has been inviting internationally famous singers and directors to their performances. The National Opera House, the first national facility for operatic performance, scheduled to open in the fall of 1997, has stage facilities of the highest level, as befitting Japan's name as the country of electronics.

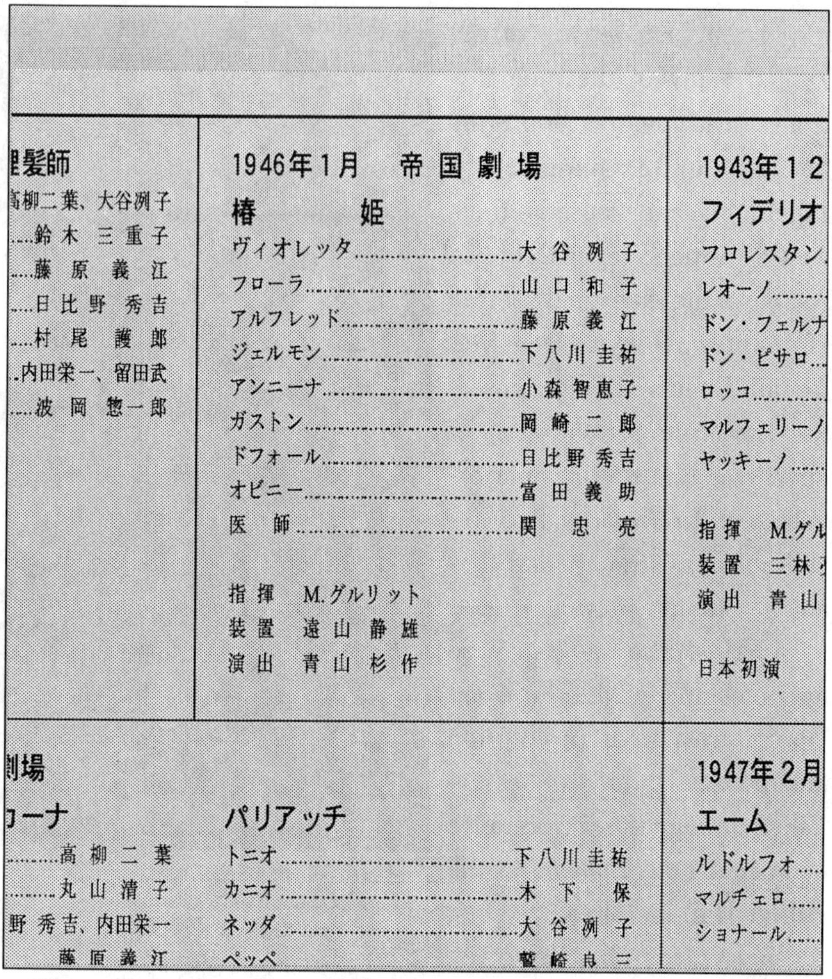

理髪師
高柳二葉、大谷洌子
...鈴木三重子
...藤原義江
...日比野秀吉
...村尾護郎
.内田栄一、留田武
...波岡惣一郎

1946年1月　帝国劇場

椿　　　姫

ヴィオレッタ	大谷洌子
フローラ	山口和子
アルフレッド	藤原義江
ジェルモン	下八川圭祐
アンニーナ	小森智恵子
ガストン	岡崎二郎
ドフォール	日比野秀吉
オビニー	富田義助
医師	関忠亮

指揮　M.グルリット
装置　遠山静雄
演出　青山杉作

1943年12
フィデリオ
フロレスタン
レオーノ
ドン・フェルナ
ドン・ピサロ
ロッコ
マルフェリーノ
ヤッキーノ

指揮　M.グル
装置　三林
演出　青山

日本初演

劇場
ーナ
........高柳二葉
....丸山清子
野秀吉、内田栄一
藤原義江

パリアッチ

トニオ	下八川圭祐
カニオ	木下保
ネッダ	大谷洌子
ペッペ	鷲崎良二

1947年2月
エーム
ルドルフォ
マルチェロ
ショナール

This portion of the Fujiwara Opera's season program is about the presentation of *Traviata* and *Fidelio,* right after World War II.

As for concerts and recitals, at least twenty with Western music programs are held in the Tokyo area each day. Many internationally famous musicians appear. Approximately every tenth day, one of the concerts is loosely related to traditional Japanese music. The use of the word concert indicates an event which presents pieces comprised of do-re-mi-fa sounds. I must confess that it is hard to recall the last time I attended a concert of purely Japanese traditional music.

The world-famous virtuosi who frequently appear on Japanese stages present operas, recitals and concerts. All the major opera

Major newspaper advertisement: The latest concert tour of Japan — the Wien Philharmonic Orchestra — conducted by Zubin Mehta (an East Indian) and Seiji Ozawa (a Japanese). The violin soloist is Midori (a Japanese). Tickets cost an average of $300 (U.S.) each and sold out swiftly.

companies and symphony orchestras from around the world perform frequently in Japan and are so popular they are even asked to repeat their presentations two or three times. Among them are New York's Metropolitan Opera, Milan's La Scala, the Berlin National Opera and the Moscow Bolshoi Opera. As for symphony orchestras, among those which come to Japan regularly are the Wien Philharmonic, New York Philharmonic, Boston Symphony, St. Petersburg Symphony, Philadelphia Symphony and the Amsterdam Concertgebouw Orchestra.

The Japanese not only enjoy listening to music, they also play it and take great pleasure in playing it. Government statistics for the mid-1990s indicate that one in three families has a piano. When you include other types of keyboards, every Japanese family has some type of Western music instrument at home. The Yamaha Corporation, which is the biggest company of its kind in Japan and the world's leading manufacturer of musical instruments, is proud of its 10~15 percent world market share of piano sales.

About two hundred full orchestras are registered in the Japan Amateur Orchestra Association and community orchestras are active all over Japan.

Choirs

One of the special musical activities in Japan is the female choirs which have been organized by music-loving women. Usually, the members are not graduates of music schools. Often they may not even have any fundamental musical training other than that of regular school music courses. In other words, these are genuine amateur activities although some of the groups present quite sophisticated programs, including concerts of works by Béla Bartók, Zoltán Kodály and other contemporary technically advanced composers.

Most of the members of such choirs are housewives. Quite naturally, such groups have been nicknamed "Mamma's Choir." Female choirs have been popular in the last twenty years. By the mid-1990s, some 1,500 such groups are registered with the All Japan Chorus League, Inc. If we include beginners' choirs that do not belong to the league, the number throughout the entire country climbs tremendously, to well over 15,000. This is a recent phenomenon partly due to changes in household technology that result in housewives having more free time. The reaction of Japanese women is to become involved in a variety of cultural activities, including singing. This is a typical dimension of musical activities in Japan today.

Generally speaking, amateur musical activities sprang from

The 18th Annual All-Japan National "Mamma's Choir" Contest

choir activities even before World War II and were quite popular in colleges and girls' high schools. These two different categories make for interesting comparisons.

By the early 1930s, the school choir activities had become widespread. College choirs consisted mainly of male voices presenting material in the style of the glee clubs of American colleges. High school choirs were usually dominated by female voices and their repertoires were different from those of the college groups. The girls sang works such as those by Stephen Foster, about the good old days in America, while the boys of the glee clubs sang European classics.

Here, it is necessary to note that Japan's school system before World War II was quite different from that which was established after the war. For instance, a coeducational system began only in 1946. Before that, when choirs were initiated, colleges were almost always exclusively for males and high schools were strictly divided

The 48th Annual All-Japan National Contest of High School Choirs

between boys' and girls' high schools. Boys in high school usually paid no attention to choirs but rather were enthusiastic about sports, particularly baseball.

The Junior High School Brass Band

Brass Bands

Another type of musical activity which is really popular in Japan is the brass band. Every junior high and high school, even elementary school, has its own brass band. The music they present is usually of quite a high level. The instruments are of professional quality and the sounds are close to that which you would expect at a major public concert. The Japan Brass Band League, Inc., holds an annual national Brass Band Contest where the standard of music is as high as that of the professionals and fine music can be heard. The final contestants present impressive music. I have had the opportunity to listen to fine music many times from the critical vantage of the jury box.

The choirs and the brass bands are the two main streams of musical activity in Japan's schools. By the mid-1990s, there was a growing trend toward the establishment of symphony orchestras in schools. In the major cities, high school students are likely to learn and play string instruments as well as brass.

Japanese Musicians Abroad

It is quite the norm to see Japanese-made automobiles in many countries nowadays. It is also quite common to find Japanese players in the orchestras of famous symphonies around the world. Tohru Yasunaga, a Japanese trained exclusively in Japan, is the concertmaster of the prestigious Berlin Philharmonic Orchestra. Boston, Philadelphia, Paris, Lyons, Amsterdam, The Hague, Rome — the orchestras of all these and other major cities include Japanese players among their leading members.

Seiji Ozawa (right) and the author in New York, 1963.

In the early 1960s, when I was a student in the United States, neither Japanese cars nor Japanese orchestral players were seen there other than Seiji Ozawa, who was then assistant conductor at the New York Philharmonic Symphony Orchestra. Now he is internationally famous and the general music director of the Boston Symphony.

To my knowledge, there must be over two hundred fifty active Japanese musicians on the concert platforms of Western countries. You will find Japanese conductors, orchestral players, pianists and operatic singers. In the 1960s, the sopranos who played in the opera *Madame Butterfly* sometimes looked so much larger than the men whom they played opposite. The woman seemed physically to overwhelm her counterpart, the handsome, skinny tenor Pinkerton. Now, in almost all the performances around the world, the opera's title role "Chocho-san" is usually taken by a Japanese soprano. No longer does the female look larger than the male.

Let me share an anecdote about Japanese musicians who perform on European stages. Several years ago, the famous Amsterdam Concertgebouw Orchestra held auditions in Tokyo to recruit string players, perhaps because the Japanese have the highest reputation in this area. Eventually, twelve violinists became members of the Dutch orchestra. Now, twelve members were a little too many. Clearly, the Japanese musicians, who were all attractive young women, were not European. A problem was created when they were seated in the front lines — it almost looked to the audience as if the orchestra was from some Asian country. Therefore, the orchestra decided to seat the violinists here and there among the rest of the musicians, in order to hide them from the audience.

Music Education

It is helpful here to know something about the educational back-ground of professional music training in Japan. We have as many as 88 music colleges and departments in Japan. Geographically, Japan is a little smaller than the state of California, which has about 25 music schools.

The institutes in Japan graduate some 10,000 students each year, which is quite a special accomplishment. Every major music school in Europe and the United States accepts Japanese students — the Paris Conservatoire, New York's Juilliard School of Music, the Curtis Institute of Music in Philadelphia, Berlin's Hochschule für Musik and the Verdi Conservatorio in Milan.

My brother, who has lived in Italy for many years, tells me that usually some 300 Japanese voice students, almost all female, stay in the Milan area. In recent years, there are as many as 1,000 in the summer months when short-term private music schools open. My brother believes that some of these schools are expressly aimed at Japanese students. Indeed, I venture to suggest that thousands of Japanese music students want to stay in Western countries and study Western music. If nothing else, this is a strong indication of the depth of feeling the people of Japan have for Western music.

The Winds of Change

The Advent of a Different System

Contemporary Japan is filled with Western music, even though this music has a history of barely a century in the country. Yet Japan may well have had an introduction to Western music considerably before this with the advent of Francisco de Xavier, the first Jesuit preacher who arrived in Japan in the mid-sixteenth century. It is recorded that he brought with him a medieval musical instrument in the lute-mandolin style. Also, the Tensho Juvenile Mission to the Vatican in the late sixteenth century, sent by the provincial feudal lords of the southern island area Kyushu, studied the string quartet. On their return to Japan, they played European music in Kyoto in the presence of the Shogun Hideyoshi.

It is clear, however, that the real introduction of do-re-mi-fa music took place in the days of the Meiji Restoration, in the 1860s. That was the time when Japan truly turned from feudal to modern ways.

The government enforced many policies, from military to the educational, based on the European systems, which were considered new and advanced.

Hundreds of bright young Japanese students were sent to learn about European culture and civilization. On the other hand, the government invited many European experts from the technologically advanced countries as counsel. These "experts" were nicknamed *o-yatoi kyoshi* and received extraordinarily high payment, as high as the salary of the prime minister of that time.

Medical doctors, law professors, language teachers, specialists in agriculture, civil engineers, educators and professionals in the fine arts were all invited to Japan. The Meiji government was quite willing to learn from all the European cultures to make Japan anew in order for it to become a country of international cultural standards.

In 1872, the government initiated an educational system. This was the first time Japan had systematic school education throughout the entire country. Previously, private institutions had independent classes which were all different. The new curricula for elementary level schools included:

1. Spelling
2. Penmanship
3. Vocabulary
4. Conversation
5. Reading (Comprehension)
6. Moral Education
7. Book Reading (Literature)
8. Grammar
9. Mathematics

10. Hygiene (Health)
11. Geography
12. Science
13. Gymnastics
14. Singing (music) *no use for the present*

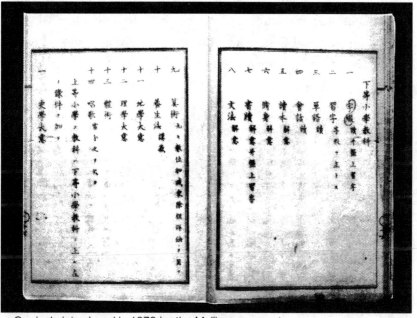

Curricula introduced in 1872 by the Meiji government.

Elementary schools were immediately built over almost all of Japan, regardless of whether in big cities or small villages. The Japanese were quite naive about the governmental decree and took the new educational policy to be exceedingly important. The new curricula were all in place in the newly built schools by 1873 except for item 14, Singing (music).

What to Teach?

Generally speaking, the Meiji government studied the cultures of England, France, Germany, Holland and the United States. Ideological theory for law and philosophy came from Germany and France; from England came practical items such as technology. The educational system came from France. It is not clear why the French educational system was chosen, but perhaps some French law professors were involved with the government so it was convenient to learn from them.

However, item 14 was a major problem, for France had established the "conservatory system" to teach music outside the regular

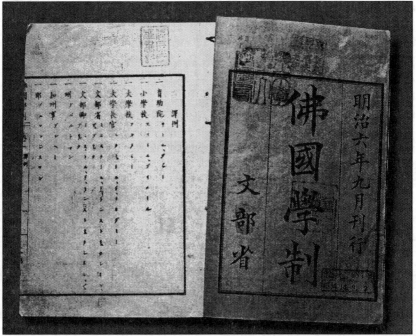

Japanese translation of material from the French educational system.

elementary school system. Thus, they were obliged to suspend the implementation of this subject. This was done by adding the phrase "no use for the present."

The Japanese acknowledged the value of fine art as an educational tool even then, but they were not versed in the ways to implement the teaching of the subject. Much discussion was held about the music. Which music would be used? Would it be Japanese traditional music or Western music? Would it be Japanese music for a nationalistic education or Western music for a new advanced culture?

Japanese traditional music (songs) are, roughly:

1. *Yoh-kyoku* — Musical accompaniment to *Noh* plays;

2. *Naga-uta* — Accompaniment to kabuki theatrical plays;

3. *Ko-uta* and its equivalent — Tea house entertainment;

4. *Warabe-uta* — Traditional children's song.

The Ministry of Education considered that numbers 1 and 2 were too sophisticated and believed that even the words were too difficult for children to understand. Number 3 was considered indecent. Thus, it was concluded that because number 4 was the easiest, it might be appropriate for the new education, even though the material was simple. It was felt that music classes centered on Japanese music would not be adequate for the new system and new era.

Ultimately, the government concluded that the music curriculum needed to be centered on Western music that contained some material for Japanese tastes. Once the decision was made, the fact was that Western music was virtually foreign to the Japanese, including government officials. Then helpful news came from a Japanese student in Boston that children's music classes had begun in the Boston area and that training courses for music teachers were also available at some schools there. The Ministry of Education asked for details from the Japanese Consulate General, which had opened in New York in 1870. Then a consul was sent by himself to Boston to gather as much information as possible.

Americans Pioneer Music Classes in Their Schools

Usually, music is not included in regular elementary school curricula in European countries. Basically, the private conservatories are the professional institutes for training musicians. Traditionally, the public schools concentrated on reading, writing and arithmetic. A few private schools enjoyed music classes. It is true that education belongs in a trinity of intellectual courses, courses of virtue and physical training — in other words, education for the brain, the heart and the body.

In this sense, the traditional European way of school education was for the brain, while the heart and the body were nourished during time after school.

Music courses at regular elementary schools were initiated in the mid-nineteenth century in the United States in the Boston area. It was a first in world history. America was a newly developed country, a vast continent being opened by pioneers. The only culture was that of the Native Americans. The culture of the European settlers had had little time to develop. Therefore, it was seen that schooling was an important cultural tool and even music should be taught in the schools.

Musical courses actually began as church singing classes. Many wanted to avoid the chaos of hymn singing during church services. Some leaders organized singing classes but these individuals were not professionally trained. In 1832, one of these, Lowell Mason (1792~1872), a self-taught musician, established the Boston Academy of Music, which was the first music teacher training school.

Lowell Mason

The school sent teachers throughout the area, even beyond New England. Lowell Mason can be called one of the initiators of music education in the U.S. public school system.

Luther Whiting Mason

Among the first graduates from the Boston Academy of Music was another Mason, Luther Whiting Mason (1824~1896, no relative to Lowell), who became an important figure in the development of Western music education in Japan.

Isawa, the Samurai

Shuji Isawa

Shuji Isawa (1851~1917) was the son of a humble *samurai* from the Takatoh province, now Nagano Prefecture, approximately in the middle of Honshu Island. He was very bright and was awarded a government scholarship. He went to Tokyo and graduated from Daigaku Nankoh, now Tokyo University. At the age of 24, he was appointed the principal of the Aichi Normal School. A year later, he received an astonishing appointment to go to the U.S. to study the educational system, with an emphasis on elementary schooling. He left Japan from Yokohama on July 18, 1875.

The Japanese Consulate General in New York recorded that Isawa went to Boston and entered the Bridgewater State Normal

The Bridgewater State Normal School in the 1990s — now a college.

School (the first state normal school in America, now a state college), where he studied for two years. He worked hard and his school scores were very good in everything except for the two subjects of English pronunciation and singing (music).

Isawa's command of English reading and writing was fairly good but his study of spoken English in Japan had not prepared him for the actual pronunciation in Boston. The first foreign language he learned was Dutch, by which he was greatly influenced. Japanese and Dutch influences on the English language — those formed a base for his English pronunciation. Isawa had a struggle to reform his English speech.

Another struggle was music.

This was the first time Isawa learned of do-re-mi-fa music.

The samurai families of feudal Japan did not consider music very important. Indeed, it was almost neglected. In addition, Isawa, the son of samurai, was unfortunately almost tone deaf. The school dean, Professor Boyden, had known of Isawa's difficulty and his cultural background and kindly offered to cancel the music — he suggested that music not be counted as a graduation credit. But Isawa's pride as a Japanese student made him reluctant to accept this offer. And by that time, Isawa had evaluated the importance of music in elementary schooling.

A. G. Boyden

The basic premise for children's education in the Boston area was strongly influenced by the Pestalozzi

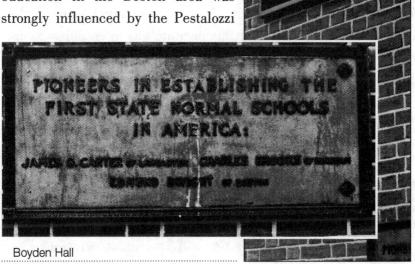

PIONEERS IN ESTABLISHING THE
FIRST STATE NORMAL SCHOOLS
IN AMERICA:

Boyden Hall

philosophy, which emphasizes the value of children's behavior. Singing (music) was apparently a valid school subject. Isawa decided to study music intensively with a private tutor, a well-known music teacher by the name of Luther Whiting Mason — yes, he was one of the two Masons of whom I have written.

Isawa studied earnestly with Mason privately for about a year. During this time, the two became fast friends — something which influenced the introduction of music education later in Japan.

Luckily, Isawa was able to obtain a basic command of Western music and obtain full credit for graduation from the Bridgewater State Normal School. When he had graduated, he wrote a special report to the Minister of Education in Tokyo: "Expectations for Implementing Singing (Music) in the New School System in Japan." He now believed firmly in the value of music in the elementary school curriculum. Isawa joined Harvard University's Department of Science where he studied for about a year. He returned to Japan in 1878.

The following year, the National Institute of Music *(Ongaku Torishirabe Gakari)* was built. Isawa was a central figure at the institute. The main task for this institute was to establish a curriculum and to prepare a textbook for singing (music) to be incorporated at elementary schools throughout Japan.

Bridgewater SNS: (from left) First School, Secondary School, and Normal Hall.

The Initiation of Music Courses in Japan

Isawa was the only Japanese who knew "what Western music is, how it is to be performed and why to teach it to children." He wanted to invite to Japan his private music tutor Luther Whiting Mason as an expert in music education to help him. Frankly speaking, the task was too great for Isawa alone.

The government acknowledged his idea and invited Mason to help Isawa to begin to incorporate into the curriculum the subject of singing (music) which they had temporarily not used. Mason was willing to accept this invitation and arrived in Tokyo in March of 1880.

The first step in their joint work was for Isawa and Mason to compile a textbook for music education. The main idea, which was acknowledged by the government, was that the music could be in the Western style but with Japanese feeling. Thus, the words and lyrics used in the textbook were to be Japanese while the musical notes were to be Western. Half the songs could be Japanese, half Western.

Isawa organized the editing committee, which included Japanese language professors and poets. Mason recommended appropriate Western songs to the committee, which discussed the sentiments: would they be good for Japanese children or not? The difficulty of putting Japanese lyrics to Western songs was also considered. The lyrics were not translations of the originals but were newly written and based on the Japanese esthetic or famous literary works.

For example, the famous Scottish folk song *Annie Laurie* was used in the textbook with the Japanese title *Saijo*, which means

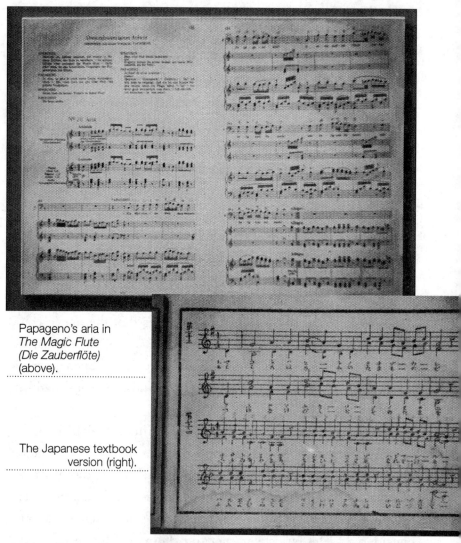

Papageno's aria in
The Magic Flute
(Die Zauberflöte)
(above).

The Japanese textbook
version (right).

"talented women." The content of the Japanese lyrics was based on
the work of two eminent women of eleventh-century literature —
Murasaki Shikibu (who wrote the famous novel *Genji Monogatari,
The Tale of Genji)* and Sei-shoh Nagon (author of the distinguished
collection of essays, *Makura no Soh-shi, The Pillow Book*).

Another amusing example is that of a foolish bird catcher, Papageno, who appears in Mozart's famous opera, *The Magic Flute (Die Zauberflöte)*. One of the most popular arias he sings is, "I'd like to have a girl friend." This was put into the textbook with the Japanese lyrics, "Sincerity is most important to human beings."

How vast the difference between the original and the textbook version!

The textbooks were designed in three volumes. Volume 1 begins with very simple music theory and thirty-one easy songs follow, one-third of which were composed by committee members (perhaps including Isawa and Mason. The composer's name is not shown on every song in the textbooks); the rest were Western melodies with decent Japanese lyrics.

In Volumes 2 and 3, the number of Western songs is increased tremendously. Songs for the higher grades were brought from the West. They came from the textbook printed in Boston that L. W. Mason himself had compiled some years before. The three volumes

The first Japanese elementary school music textbook, published in 1881.

of the textbook include ninety-one songs and, to my eyes, about 20 percent were of Japanese taste. Volume 1 of the music textbook was released in November 1881. Historically, it was the first Japanese music book printed with Western music notations but the words in Japanese. Volume 2 came out in 1883 and 3 was released in 1884. Isawa's efforts to start "music" as an elementary school subject took a step forward.

The National Institute of Music (Ongaku Torishirabe Gakari) was in the process of training twenty-two students (nine males and thirteen females) to be teachers of music; the institute was

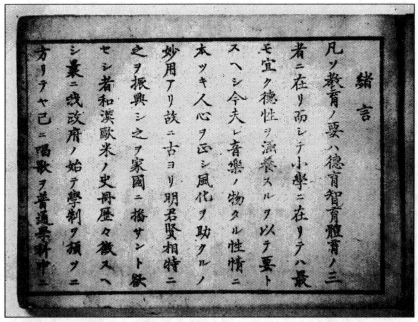

Preface to textbook: The key to education consists of a trinity of intellectual courses, courses in morals and physical training. At the elementary school level, courses in morals are very important. Music is effective for giving the correct idea to humanity and creating happiness. Many great and wise masters have promoted music throughout world history regardless of nationality, Eastern or Western. With the introduction of the new school system, the government will include music as one of the subjects of elementary school courses . . . ."

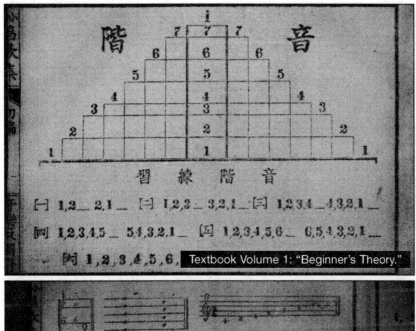
Textbook Volume 1: "Beginner's Theory."

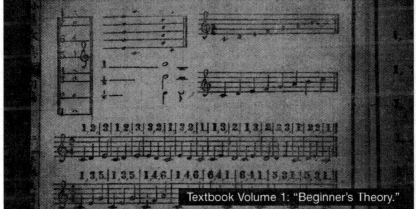
Textbook Volume 1: "Beginner's Theory."

also compiling texts other than the three noted here. At the same time, Mason was trying to teach Japanese children at the elementary school that belonged to the Tokyo Normal School and the kindergarten of the Tokyo Women's Normal School. The responses of Japanese children to the Western music material was also being studied.

Despite the adults' feelings of embarrassment, the young

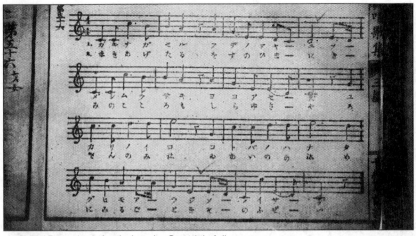

Saijo: Based on *Annie Laurie,* Scottish folk song.

teachers and children reacted very well, even enjoying the subject. It seemed to the personnel of the Institute of Music that the results were good. The Meiji Empress even visited the Tokyo Women's Normal School to see the new method of music education and she was really impressed.

A wall chart of music was released with Volume 1 of the music text. The wall chart was quite a convenient teaching aid, created

Chu-shin, Loyal Warrior: Based on *Juanita,* Spanish folk song.

The first Japanese organ (harmonium) made by Yamaha.

by Mason himself. At the Paris Exposition of 1879, it was awarded a prize as an effective educational tool.

So far, Volume 1 of the textbook and the wall chart were prepared and the teachers were all trained in Japan. But there was a major difficulty: musical instruments were needed. The ten square pianos (a unique, transitional model between the classic grand and the upright; the strings were set on the diagonal) at the institute came with Mason from the U.S. The piano was an expensive instrument for a regular elementary school. The koto, the Japanese harp, was tried but this did not work because the traditional koto tuning is very different from that of do-re-mi-fa.

Isawa and Mason remembered the scene at the service in a tiny church back in New England — an organ with a foot pedal system. The correct name was harmonium, and it was far cheaper than a piano. Soon, because of their recommendation, every normal school was equipped with a harmonium.

The first Japanese harmonium was made by Torakusu Yamaha (the founder of the Yamaha Corporation) in 1887 on Isawa's advice. It helped lower the price of harmoniums in Japan. In several years, almost all the elementary schools around Japan were equipped with harmoniums. (The first Japanese-made piano appeared in 1899.) In 1887, the National Institute of Music became the National Music School and Isawa was appointed its president.

As for L. W. Mason, he taught at some prestigious schools, including the School of Peers (Gakushuin). He returned home to Boston in 1887 on the expiration of his contract. Although he certainly wanted to return to Japan, the Japanese government did not renew the contract.

Two Composers

In the early years of Japanese music history in the Western sense, two composers are unforgettable: Rentaro Taki (1879~1903) and Kohsaku Yamada (1886~1965). They were really the pioneers and founders of do-re-mi-fa composition in Japan.

Rentaro Taki was the first graduate majoring in piano at the Tokyo National Music School (now the National Fine Arts University, Music Department). He continued his study at Leipzig Music College in Germany on a governmental scholarship. He studied mainly music composition here, for he possessed the idea that he would write contemporary Japanese music.

At the age of nineteen, when he was a student at the Tokyo National Music School, he wrote a song,

Rentaro Taki

日　本　男　児

東　郊 作歌
瀧 廉太郎 作曲

にっ ぱん だん じ そ は な に ぞ に
っ ぱん だん じ そ は たれ ぞ たい ほう
しょう じゅう な に か ある しょう えん だん う も
な に か ある い き の ね た ゆる ふ え の ね
は き えても き えず きみ が な は

Japanese Boy by Rentaro Taki.

Japanese Boy, which is his oldest existing composition. The time of this composition was a little after the Japanese victory over feudal China during the Sino-Japan War (1894~95); the title reflects this. Taki wanted to describe the strength and sturdiness of the Japanese boy.

Taki wrote many simple compositions for nursery songs even before his departure for Germany. He went to Leipzig in 1901 and qualified as a student at the Leipzig National Conservatory but unfortunately he could not complete his studies. The following year, he was ordered to return to Japan by the government because of his illness, tuberculosis. Taki died in 1903 at the early age of twenty-five.

Menuet
(Minuet)

Rentaro Taki

瀧廉太郎 作曲

Menuet – page 2

Menuet – page 3

....

Consequently, the body of his work is relatively small, about fifty: two piano pieces, seven choir pieces and songs as well as seventeen simple songs for pre-school children.

Kohsaku Yamada was only seventeen years younger than Taki but we need to know that the musical circumstances in Japan during his time were different from those of previous years. In other words, westernization in Japan had accelerated to a high tempo. Several years meant far more than that in the cultural development of that era in Japan.

Kohsaku Yamada, who preferred to write his name in the French way, Koçak, was also a graduate of the Tokyo National Music School, where he majored in vocal music. (After graduation he went to the Berlin Hochschule für Musik, Germany, to study composition.)

Kohsaku Yamada

There were only two courses: instrumental music and vocal. The school's composition course did not appear until 1932.

Undeterred, Yamada pursued a wide range of studies by himself. He played piano and cello. He was an important member of the school orchestra, the principal cellist. Luckily, I was given the opportunity to listen to his live piano playing when I was a boy. To my ears, his skill was professional, and I was quite excited at the live performance of a great master.

Yamada was a fine conductor, too. He appeared on the podium of Carnegie Hall conducting the New York Philharmonic Orchestra in 1918. This was the first time a Japanese musician had so performed.

Yamada's works are numerous and cover many categories of music, from grand opera to piano pieces, from art songs to nursery songs. His songs are considered the most important creations among his works. Not only did Yamada initiate the study of music for vocal students but he is also responsible for the first step in the introduction of Western music to Japan, the introduction of Western style songs.

We needed many good simple songs to suit the prevailing taste for Western music in Japan. The few additional Japanese musicians who composed "authentic" Western style music, even though they were barely eligible to do so, wrote children's songs.

Children's Songs in Japan

I would like to explain more about Japanese children's songs, for such songs have an interesting historical background. "Children's songs" is a straight translation of the Japanese words *kodomo-no uta,* or songs for children. It is not exactly the same as the word nursery song or nursery rhyme. A nursery rhyme is usually a song to be sung by pre-school children or sung to little children. It is closer to cradle song. If I define children's song as the equivalent of babies' songs, it might be too narrow. Children's songs in Japanese has a wide meaning and is a common expression.

As noted, Western music was introduced in the course of Japanese cultural modernization about a hundred years ago.

According to the governmental decree of the new educational system, music was apparently one of the elementary school subjects and music was a required part of the culture. A school music textbook was prepared and published in 1881. This particular book is titled *shoh-ka* (a simple translation is "singing song"), and those songs compiled in the book were called shoh-ka as well.

Although many of those melodies were derived from Western folk songs, the words were original and purely Japanese. The words described traditional virtues, loyalty to the master and the beautiful landscapes of Japan. Those were the interesting combinations of Western folk tunes and the conventional ingredients of Japanese words. Educators at that time conceived that songs sung for educational purposes should be serious ones.

The words contained the slogan of the cultural restoration quite often. (Some of the words and music of the songs in the textbook were originally written by Japanese educators of that time.) Shoh-ka is designed to be sung by children, so shoh-ka was taken as children's song.

This is the origin of the Japanese terminology "children's songs" in the Japanese language. It is quite understandable that the words of school text songs are inclined to be moralistic or square.

About twenty years after the first edition of the music textbook was released, around the start of the twentieth century, Japanese poets and educators were beginning to say that in addition to shoh-ka, more artistic songs for children were needed, or at least songs with words that children could easily relate to and understand. Then, the new "artistic songs for children" movement was started.

They called this movement *Akai Tori* ("The Red Bird") children's song movement.

The key person in this movement was Mie-kichi Suzuki, a novelist and editor. Many composers, poets and writers collaborated under this flag. They called these new children's songs *doh-yoh*. Doh-yoh is the Japanese name for children's songs that have different ingredients from shoh-ka.

Shoh-ka and Doh-yoh

As I have mentioned, there are two different groups of Japanese children's songs historically.

1. Shoh-ka, which appeared in the first edition of the school textbook of 1881.
2. Doh-yoh, which appeared in the 1910s, is the counterproduct to sho-ka, which tends to be moralistic.

It is interesting to realize that Taki and Yamada are closely connected to each group as composers: Taki to the first, shoh-ka; Yamada to the second, doh-yoh.

Rentaro Taki composed seventeen songs for pre-school children. They were published in 1901 in Tokyo under the title, *Yohchi-en Shoh-ka (Kindergarten Shoh-ka)*. These are the first Japanese songs with piano accompaniments for little children. Taki also wrote some children's songs even before this but they were pure melody, there were no accompaniments. These yohchi-en sho-ka were commissioned by the Tokyo Women's Normal School Kindergarten, the first kindergarten in Japan. Taki carefully composed these songs so that they would not be too difficult for kindergarten teachers to play, for usually the teachers were not professionally trained as musicians.

These are the first original songs for the early childhood of the Japanese: *"Nightingale," "Skylark Sings," "Carp Streamer," "On the Ocean," "Momo-taro"* (the title of a popular Japanese fairy tale), *"A Frog in a Pond," "Squirt-Gun."* These titles of yohchi-en shoh-ka indicate the style of the works.

水 あ そ び

龍廉太郎 作歌・作曲

Squirt-Gun: Lyrics and music by Rentaro Taki

The content of the words is quite different from the sho-ka published in 1881, for the yohchi-en shoh-ka are not moralistic and have free expression and pure artistic feeling.

Musically, they are quite interesting too. Fifteen songs out of seventeen were composed to pentatonic scale. Pentatonic scale (a scale having five tones to an octave, as the five black keys of a piano octave), is quite common among Japanese folk songs and

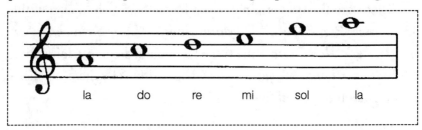

almost all traditional Japanese nursery rhymes are set to this scale.

When considering sound susceptibility, Taki chose the pentatonic scale for writing songs for young children. Some children's games which were originally designed to be yohchi-en shoh-ka may reasonably be placed between shoh-ka and doh-yoh. Had Rentaro Taki lived longer, he might have added some variety to his children's song catalog. He left us too early.

Kohsaku Yamada was a versatile composer. He wrote various types of music but we cannot overlook his children's songs, especially *Doh-Yoh Hyakkyoku-Shu (One Hundred Songs for Children)*, which was published in Tokyo from 1927 to 1929 in consecutive years.

When you compare Taki's children's songs to Yamada's, you will see some major differences in composition technique and artistic maturity, even though the purposes of the two are different.

Taki's works were a kind of pilot presentation during the early stages of Western music in Japan. The simplicity must be appreciated and the game to play with the song must have been appropriate, for they became popular quite rapidly.

Yamada's works were more mature than Taki's, because he had spent more time in Europe developing his technique than Taki. Yamada was really able to study the twentieth-century way of music composition. In other words, Taki studied Mozart and Beethoven whereas Yamada studied Brahms and Wagner.

Taki's children's songs came out in 1901 and Yamada's came out in 1926. During this space of twenty-five years, the Japanese made tremendous progress in familiarizing themselves with and acquiring Western culture — much greater than the transition of babies to adults.

Kono-Michi, This Road:
Music by Kohsaku Yamada, from *One Hundred Songs For Children*.

As a composer, Yamada was one of the Akai Tori movement's leading collaborators. He had specific ideas when composing children's songs. He wrote in the November 1922 edition of the magazine *Shi-to-Ongaku (Poetry and Music):*

> There are two different types of children's songs. The artistic children's song and the song where children play (game song). When a song flatters children, it might be possible to create immediate excitement or enjoyment. But there is neither artistic growth nor afterglow and, of course, no artistic contentment. Excitement will vanish in a moment. My works are not like that. My children's songs might be a little difficult for children to understand at first, but they are important milestones to lead them to the real beauty of music. My works for children may be called educative or humanistic.

His songs for children, over 200 pieces, became not only musical treasures for Japanese children but good models even for artistic songs by the composers who followed after Yamada.

Taki and Yamada were pioneers whose compositions have been exceptionally important to modern Japanese culture. Taki acted in the opening role for Yamada, who was able to greatly expand his role as the second contributor.

In the final analysis we understand that first, Western music was introduced to Japan as children's songs, shoh-ka, in the school textbook of 1881. Taki and Yamada built the foundation for modern Japanese musical creation by composing many beautiful children's songs.

It can therefore be said that modern Japanese music as well as the musical life of Japan were based on children's songs.

Maestro Ferdinand Beyer

The name of the composer-pianist Ferdinand Beyer (1803~1863) is not as well-known as his contemporary, Beethoven (1770~1827). Both were born in Germany. The name Beyer, however, is very popular in Japan. Even a five-year-old who does not know Beethoven at all recognizes Beyer easily. There may not be

Piano works by Ferdinand Beyer.

another country in the world where Maestro Beyer is as famous as in Japan.

The name of the Bayer aspirin is known internationally, but in Japan this name is renowned for the piano method and the textbook, *Beyer, Vorschule Im Klavierspiel, opus 101.* I have seen some of Beyer's compositions, easy piano pieces, included in many beginner textbooks around the world. However, I have never seen this particular text outside Japan.

Beyer is widely used for beginner piano lessons in Japan. Not only is Beyer popular among Japanese children but it is a very important textbook in music education, especially at teacher training institutes. At many teachers' colleges, Beyer is used to introduce piano technique and it is also the choice for designated pieces

Beginner's textbooks by Ferdinand Beyer.

of the government examination for nursery school teachers almost all over Japan.

Maestro Beyer was also something of a popular pianist in his time. He was a guest at many salons in high society. He might play famous pieces by Haydn and Mozart as well as his own compositions, which were created for a salon's particular atmosphere. I have his piano pieces which I bought at an antique bookstore in Vienna. These are gay pieces in a light style, typical European salon music in which I found melodies from famous operas and pop tunes of the era. I suspect these pieces were written to entertain salon guests.

Beyer's work for piano — I haven't seen anything other than piano pieces — is the type of music that is easy to play. Even an amateur pianist will enjoy playing them. Beyer was a pianist and, as is quite often the case, a good piano teacher, which is how he wrote this type of composition. Maestro Beyer was a music professor, too.

Why Is Beyer So Popular in Japan?

Enthusiasm for Beyer exists because the majority of Japanese children take piano lessons; also, there is some kind of keyboard instrument in almost all Japanese homes now. These phenomena started after World War II. In 1945, when the war ended, culturally thirsty Japanese wanted to drink deeply of the wine of civilized pursuits, not available during the war years.

One of the most appreciated wines was Western music. Before the war, even during the war, intellectual Japanese were fond of listening to Western music. It didn't matter whether it was classical or popular.

The piano was accepted as a symbol both of Western music and culture for many years in Japan.

Immediately after the war, symphony concerts became more popular than before and the subscription tickets to the concerts sold out swiftly.

In 1955, when The Symphony of the Air (the former NBC Symphony Orchestra) came to hold concerts in Tokyo, the first symphony orchestra from abroad after the war, the line of people wishing to buy tickets was a whole kilometer long.

At about the time of the Korean War, Japan's economy had improved, as had the living standard of the Japanese. It was at this time that Japanese parents began to involve their children in music lessons at an early age. The Japanese concept of the enjoyment of music through listening evolved to become the enjoyment of music by playing music. One good example is the Suzuki method for violin which began in Japan. It is generally accepted that the Jews and Japanese are two of the most educationally-minded people. Next to food is education: next to reading, writing and arithmetic, music will be fine — this might be their national way of thinking.

While living rather humbly, Japanese parents were likely to buy a piano for their children to play, even though it is expensive. I think it is a special scene: a piano standing next to a refrigerator in the small living room of a modest home. But it happened in Japan at that time. We called that the "music lesson boom," or the "piano lesson boom." The main educational backbone of the boom was Beyer, which even before the war had been the Bible of piano lessons for piano teachers in Japan. It was a beautiful sight to see, a mother accompanying her little daughter who held a large Beyer text tucked under her tiny arm.

Beyer seemed to be a symbol of peaceful Japan.

The Beyer Method in Japan

Now let me tell you when and how Beyer was introduced to Japan before the Meiji era. I believe that it was at the time of the Meiji Restoration that Western music as we presently appreciate it was introduced.

Professor Shuji Isawa, who graduated from Bridgewater Normal School, was certainly the first Japanese who mastered Western music and music education. When he was appointed as the director of the National Institute of Music (Ongaku Torishirabe Gakari), he recommended to the government that L. W. Mason (Isawa's private music teacher when he was studying at Bridgewater) be invited to be a professor at the institute.

Luther Mason was one of the important figures in the early days of American music education. He was quite active in promoting music education and also was an influential educator in America at that time. He came to Japan in 1880 and taught at the institute for about two years.

Luther Mason is the person who brought twenty copies of Beyer to Japan, together with ten square pianos made in America. He also brought other piano texts such as Czerny, Clementi and Kuhlau, but they were for more advanced courses.

Apparently, this innovative man had the idea that Beyer is the best piano text for beginners. Why did he choose Beyer? Setsuko Mori, a researcher at the Documentation Center for Modern Japanese Music, wrote in her study of this:

> When L. W. Mason visited European countries in 1872 looking for good educational material, he happened to find a Beyer text (the B. Schott edition, Germany). He thought it enjoyable and convenient for piano beginners.

Luckily, the English version (by a different title, *Elementary Instruction Book for Piano,* C. Prufer edition, Boston) was available in America. Mason used it in his piano class and the material was widely accepted because of his influence. It is possible that the light style of Beyer's music was favored by Mason because it avoided boring practice. Mason probably thought that Beyer would be good material for the rapid training of elementary music teachers in Japan.

Some points of value about Beyer in the beginner training are:
1. Effective method for fundamental finger training;
2. Shows good examples of functional harmonizations, which are the most important factors of Western music. These are well arranged, from simple ones to advanced steps;
3. Beyer is a good entrance to the history of classical music literature;
4. Beyer has a collection of solid examples of musical classics.

The National Institute of Music has been the Tokyo University of the Fine Arts, Music Department, for about a hundred years now. In accordance with the change in the music life of the Japanese, certainly there is much enjoyment for do-re-mi-fa music.

The piano has been given a very important place in Japanese music education, in teacher training and as a tool for teaching. Thus, Beyer has enjoyed a leading position for quite a long time. The piano lesson boom after World War II might be thought of as a reflection of the early days of the introduction of do-re-mi-fa to Japan.

About a hundred years ago, Japan imported Western music as one of the symbols of an advanced Western culture. Nearly the same situation occurred in music education with the use of Beyer. It is an interesting phenomenon that the Japanese musical trend has been so strongly influenced by America, from the use of Beyer to rock 'n' roll music.

Beyer Now

How is the Beyer textbook used in Japan? Is Beyer in the mainstream of piano lessons in Japan now? Roughly speaking, yes. The publishers of Beyer are enjoying sales of over 30,000 texts annually in Japan. However, we must understand that few piano teachers start beginner students with only that text. They also use other materials such as the French (Methode Rose), and the American (Thompson) as well as Japanese texts together with Beyer. I agree that many Japanese piano teachers are still taking Beyer as the convenient, conventional fundamentals of beginner's piano lesson. In other words, they use Beyer as the main text and the rest as enrichment.

This is the influence of the remarkable change in musical circumstances in Japan, especially after World War II. Japanese teachers were stimulated by the many music educational materials, including textbooks and methods, that were introduced in the postwar years. At that time, the Japanese teachers were receiving a wide perspective of piano lesson material and recognizing that restricting lessons to Beyer would only narrow a student's music experience.

I would like to detail some of the weak points in Beyer:

1. A lack of pieces containing counterpoint study, one of the most important musical techniques;

2. The musical expression is restricted in the so-called style of Beethoven's day of salon music;

3. Tonality is quite limited (flat keys are only in F major and B flat major, minor keys are few — 90 percent of them are in C minor);

4. Few of Beyer's pieces will be of interest to children's tastes today.

Because of these weak points, I have to explain an important aspect in the use of Beyer, and that is the change of the times, the tremendous change in musical life from the time when Beyer was introduced to Japan.

Piano lessons are more than merely learning "how to play the piano." Piano lessons are a great introduction to all music.

Consider the difference in musical circumstances even between the 1940s (immediately after the war) and the 1990s. We did not have devices such as televisions, compact discs, videos and so on, all of which are now commonplace.

The musical opportunities that children and adults now have available are highly sophisticated. The Metropolitan Opera and Michael Jackson come to Japan. Children can enjoy such shows routinely, even when at home and watching television.

I think it is rather difficult now to teach piano to Japanese children with only Beyer, an early nineteenth-century product, despite its tremendous contribution to the first introduction of do-re-mi-fa music to Japan. Japanese piano teachers today are making efforts to give children quality piano lessons which are enriched by various kinds of musical stimulation.

Japanese piano teachers are quite eager to study new material and trends in music. In this sense, composers are good coordinators for piano lessons. I believe that few countries enjoy as many children's piano pieces created by contemporary composers as in Japan. At least 300 series of such textbooks by Japanese composers are available in Japan.

Music teachers and piano tutors in Japan are musicians whose ideas are generally fairly advanced. They advise composers about the writing of piano pieces for children. However, I have to mention one important fact: the government exam for nursery school teachers (which is different from the exam for kindergarten teachers). This exam often requires candidates to finish all the Beyer numbers.

Many of the teacher training colleges in Japan require piano beginner courses mainly based on Beyer. Therefore, all such students need to pass the curriculum for the license anyway. I understand this is one of the historical legacies of Beyer from the very beginning of Japanese music education. When we consider the musical circumstances of today's Japanese children, the importance or the utility of the college practice of Beyer is minor.

The songs which are taught at nursery school or in grade school may be too hard for those who have finished only the Beyer pieces. Today, children's songs contain many musical factors: jazzy rhythms, harmonies, modern idioms. In other words, they are neither the music of Beyer's time nor of the era when Beyer was introduced to Japan. Beyer is different from the musical taste of today's children. I'd like to say something about the use of Beyer as a textbook for piano lessons which include teacher training. I agree with the premise that Beyer is one of the better piano methods. But it should be taken only as fundamental for the study of classical piano techniques of its era. It is, of course, evident that good piano teachers in Japan are using

One of the most popular contemporary piano works for children.

おねむのぞうさん
The Sleepy Elephant

服部公一 作曲
Koh-ichi Hattori

ザルツブルクのお城 (I)
Salzburg Castle

服部公一 作曲
Koh-ichi Hattori

Some pieces from
Little Poets collection

other contemporary material besides that of Beyer in their classes. Beyer is often used to supplement other methods. A hundred years ago, it was fine material to introduce do-re-mi-fa music to Japan, at a time when Western music was quite foreign. In this sense, Mason was correct, for it would have been difficult to find a better method and text than Beyer at that time.

As time passes, the position of Beyer in the musical world has changed. Many well-planned and convenient methods for beginners have been developed.

We need those that are appropriate for our time.

Today, although Beyer needs to be taken as a classic piano fundamental, it is material that has a limited use.

I have mentioned that Beyer is still required for the Japanese government exam. This creates problems among teachers who pass the exam. They eventually realize they cannot play even the nursery songs in the classroom. This is a side effect of the Beyer technique. Fortunately, there are many good methods and textbooks for every grade now.

We can find excellent textbooks for any purpose. Indeed, a number of fine piano teachers have even compiled their own texts.

Maestro Ferdinand Beyer, and the textbook Beyer, have almost completed their task in Japan.

This is an appropriate period for the government department responsible for developing material for the examination of school teachers to consider changing from the use of Beyer and moving to a contemporary method.

Music in the Educational System

Generally, Japanese children enter kindergarten at the age of four and attend for two years, then go to elementary school for six years. Next is junior high school for three years, followed by senior high school, also for three years. From grades one to nine, elementary school through junior high, education is compulsory.

The Education Law provides that music is compulsory in grades one to nine and must be taught for at least one hour per week during the school day. Even in kindergarten, music is taken as a major subject, although it is mainly singing along and simple dancing to singing. At high school, music is taken at the student's choice, as an elective subject.

At the elementary school level, music education is quite thorough. It aims to help develop some enjoyment of music and also prepares students for sol-fa, the reading and writing of music. Youngsters learn to play simple music instruments such as the recorder, xylophone and some type of keyboard. Usually, they play in ensembles in their classes. Frequently, kindergarten children take private music lessons which make their classroom activities even more enjoyable.

Japanese students have good reputations abroad for their command of music. One hears of pupils who transfer to schools in other countries in the middle of elementary school who create quite a reaction at their fine command of music, especially the reading of music. As noted previously, many countries do not include music in the elementary school curriculum. Nonetheless, it is clear from the example of Japan's inclusion of music at the lower academic levels that it is beneficial for students. A number of books discuss the beneficial ways in which music stimulates the brain and also the ability to learn as well as providing youngsters with an appropriate outlet for their feelings and energy.

As well as regular music lessons in school, music club activities are very popular in Japan. Every junior high and high school has a choir and a brass band and frequently an orchestra. Undoubtedly, even elementary schools will eventually introduce

Junior high school marching band.

similar activities. The unavoidable conclusion is that from a world perspective, music education in Japanese schools is advanced when compared to the educational systems of other nations.

National music contests are held annually in Japan for school clubs, choirs and brass bands. Those who are awarded top medals play on a level virtually identical to that of professionals. Naturally, students who go on to college usually have already had the experience of music in their high school days and so it is a normal sequence for them to continue music club activities in college, which usually has choirs, brass bands and orchestras with high standards.

Colleges often invite professional conductors to lead their orchestras and groups. Frequently, college podiums are occupied by internationally distinguished conductors. Tokyo's Sophia University Orchestra was proud to be directed by Maestro Herbert von Karajan. The programs of the concerts presented by colleges contain sophisticated pieces by composers such as Richard Strauss, Gustav Mahler and Igor Stravinsky, as well as contemporary works. There's no question about it, these works are technically exceedingly difficult to play.

Interestingly enough, the colleges are likely to commission some of today's composers to create original scores for them, and also to produce compact discs of their performances for the general market. Naturally, composers view this favorably for it is rare for commercial firms to purchase and record contemporary pieces.

A Glance at
Japanese Tradition

It is not a simple task to find a suitable definition for Japanese musics as the range is considerable and varied. We have the music of the various provinces, each with its own special flavor, and music from the different historic eras. Traditional Japanese music — which is what we will call the music enjoyed throughout the country from well before the Meiji Restoration — can be divided into several groups. The two main streams are *gagaku* and *shoh-myo*.

Gagaku

The origin of gagaku, which was initiated on the Chinese mainland, is wreathed in the mists of antiquity. Probably, it was introduced to Japan between the fifth and ninth centuries. It has been carefully preserved by the royal court of Japan. One orchestra

Gagaku concert at the Royal Palace in Tokyo.

plays gagaku exclusively. Certain families related to the court were designated to preserve and practice gagaku. For instance, the playing of *shoh*, one of the gagaku reed instruments, is handed down through the male side of a family, from father to son to grandson.

Gagaku concerts are occasionally held at the court theaters in Tokyo and the Kasuga Shrine in Nara. The concerts are not particularly connected to the royal family's schedule. The orchestra is quite adaptable, for at royal banquets they will alternate the playing of gagaku with the national anthem of the guest of honor. They can quite literally switch from the Japanese style to that of a Western orchestra and perform background music during the banquet. Anything from Mozart's minuets to waltzes by Johann Strauss

Gagaku Musical Instruments

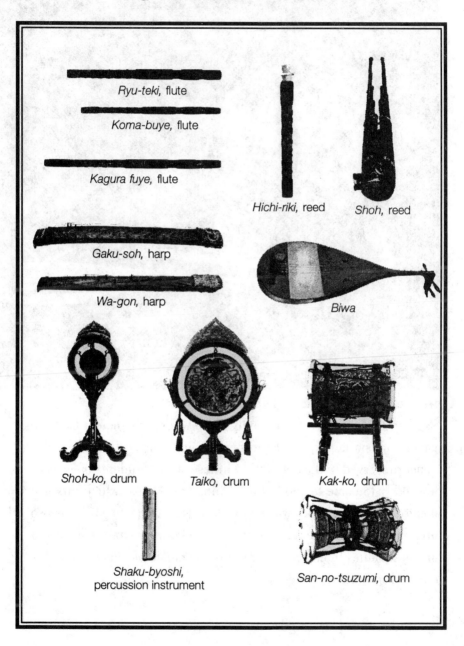

Ryu-teki, flute

Koma-buye, flute

Kagura fuye, flute

Hichi-riki, reed

Shoh, reed

Gaku-soh, harp

Wa-gon, harp

Biwa

Shoh-ko, drum

Taiko, drum

Kak-ko, drum

Shaku-byoshi,
percussion instrument

San-no-tsuzumi, drum

The Tendai shoh-myo Onritsu Institute Choir led by Rev. Umeoka.

will be performed gracefully and professionally.

The Japanese court is the only place where the ancient Chinese gagaku music is played. Elsewhere, gagaku music in Japan today is not preserved in the authentic Chinese style. Students of gagaku are likely to come to Japan from China and Korea, which are also countries where gagaku was enjoyed. It is said that gagaku has two origins: one is continental, the other Korean, where traces of gagaku music remain. In essence, gagaku is the music of the court and is enjoyed in limited circles.

Shoh-myo

Developed through the chanting of Buddhist sutras of ancient days, Buddhist priests still chant shoh-myo the way it was done hundreds of years ago. Conversely, shoh-myo has influenced numerous musical areas, primarily Japanese singing. *Ha-uta, ko-uta, gidayu-bushi* and *kiyomoto* (the school names of the different styles of singing) can be traced back a hundred years. Ultimately, all are connected to shoh-myo either fundamentally or as it

The Rev. Umeoka leading a presentation of Shoh-myo.

offshoots. It can be said that the musical elements of shoh-myo have been transmuted into the basic sense of Japanese music.

To repeat an important point, contemporary Japan is filled with do-re-mi-fa music. However, the melody lines of certain popular songs are closely related to traditional music, especially shoh-myo sounds. We call this type of popular music *enka*. One might say that these melody lines are the offspring of language inflections which bridge the differences between enka and shoh-myo.

What Are the Traditions in Japanese Contemporary Music?

So far, we have noted the preservation by the Japanese court of gagaku, the music from ancient China. Mention has also been made of shoh-myo, the chant of Buddhist sutras whose influence is discerned even in Japanese popular tunes. Now comes a description of how traditional music is used in the contemporary Japanese artistic work.

Japanese music composition following the Meiji Restoration began with the writing of simple children's songs. These were included in the first music textbook published in 1881 by the government. The songs composed were almost Western, although even then, it was clear that there was a mix or blend of Western and Japanese music as background to Japanese lyrics. First, proficiency in Western musical idioms was needed. Then came the mix or blend. The leading Japanese composer of that era was Rentaro Taki (see pages 43~56).

At the beginning of the twentieth century, several students of composition had traveled to Europe. There they came under the influence of Impressionism, which was then in vogue, works by Debussy, Ravel and Richard Strauss. Such music was quite different from the classical compositions, which might have lent themselves more easily to a blending with traditional Japanese sound. Apparently the leader among Japanese composers who studied in Europe at that time was Kohsaku Yamada (see pages 43~56).

It was not until the 1930s that original compositions using Japanese musical idioms would appear. At the start of the twentieth century, Japanese composers were mostly following Western music style and writing in imitation of Westerners. Few were able to capture the true essence of Japan in their work. Three composers, however, reflected the spirit of their country in their music and were doing so even before World War II.

> **Michio Miyagi** (1894~1956) started his career as a koto virtuoso. He composed primarily koto music in combination with other Japanese instruments and used many Japanese idioms such as traditional scales and melodies in his work.
> **Saburo Moroi** (1903~1977) studied composition at the Berlin Hochschule für Musik. He composed music in the traditional Japanese spirit.
> **Yoritsune Matsudaira** (1907~   ) started as a pianist and played modern French pieces. His compositions were based on gagaku and were the first in Japan to attempt this.

It could be said that a great deal of Japanese art music was born after World War II. Musical creation has been renewed with each new cultural stream. Fresh approaches came from around the world — the so-called 12-tone music system (the dodecaphony music initiated by Arnold Schönberg), atonal music, *musique concrète* and so on. The young composers of Japan experienced them all immediately after World War II.

Three composers in particular are important in music history.

Ikuma Dan (1924~)composed the most popular opera in Japan, *Yu-zuru (The Crane In the Dusk).* He has also written five symphonies as well as nursery songs. His music is not particularly filled with traditional Japanese sound but his basic ideas focus on his country. In 1996, Dan wrote the libretto and composed the opera *Susanoo,* which is based on the legend of the family of a Japanese emperor.

Ikuma Dan

Yasushi Akutagawa (1925~ 1989) is the composer acknowledged for creating work with Western sound. He composed a large body of symphonic music and a number of film scores. He is the composer who introduced depth and perspective to the sensibility of sound.

Yasushi Akutagawa

Toshiro Mayuzumi (1929~) is internationally known. His work is significant as much for its inclusion of the traditional philosophy of Japan as for its sound. He studied shoh-myo extensively and this is reflected in his music.

Toshiro Mayuzumi

One must also remember the composer **Yoshiro Irino** (1921~1980), who introduced dodecaphony music to Japan and composed entirely in this methodology. In this sense, he was an experimentalist in a new dimension.

The number of art music creations in Japan rose significantly after World War II, compared with what had been done up to that time. You could say that music composition in the Western sense was firmly established by the mid-1940s. Since then, the creation of art music has developed in many directions.

Electronic music is one of these innovations. One world-famous technique is a Japanese specialty. **Isao Tomita** (1932~   ), a composer of this type of music, is extremely popular. His works on compact discs occupy a full shelf in music stores in centers like New York.

We are also proud of **Tohru Takemitsu** (1930~1996), one of the most important composers of this century. He left many different types of compositions, from symphonic music to popular tunes. His importance is his unique esthetic of building music. In particular, he combined Eastern and Western sounds. In other words, he specifically designed music using Japanese instruments (which are, of course, of Chinese origin); such sounds would frequently emerge in the middle of Western symphonic orchestral music. His masterpiece *November Steps* is one of these superb blends. Takemitsu did not conceive of music in a way that limited it to being

Tohru Takemitsu

either Eastern or Western, Asian or European. Rather, he would consider the roots of music and then merge disparate sounds and sensibilities as well as instruments into a unified, single magnificent opus.

We Japanese composers endeavor to follow in the steps of Takemitsu. New music needs to be built on traditional Japanese sound, which has evolved in various directions, some more successfully than others. Some composers start with folk melodies, others begin with philosophies. I believe, finally, that Takemitsu integrated everything in his works.

As we move into the twenty-first century, Japan's world of music has a rich heritage for our future creations and performances.

Index

About the Author

Koh-ichi Hattori, one of Japan's fore-most composers, has had his compo-sitions published and played around the world. A well-known commentator on Japanese television and in other media on the subjects of the fine arts and education, he is a professor at the Tokyo Kasei University's Graduate School and also lectures at the Gakushuin University.

Involved in a wide range of musical endeavors for decades, he has been sent by the Japan Foundation on governmental international cultural activities to many countries to lecture and introduce the contemporary life of the Japanese from the focus of music. The international projects with which he has been associated have been presented in many different countries, including the United States, the United Kingdom, Germany, Italy, France, Russia, Australia, Argentina, Brazil, China and Korea.

Professor Hattori was born in Yamagata, Japan in 1933 and studied at Gakushuin University in Tokyo, the Berlin Music College in Germany and Michigan State University in the United States. The recipient of numerous awards, including the Asia Foundation Grant (1962), the Disc Grand Prize of Japan (1965), the Governmental Art Prize (1974, 1983) and the Foreign Minister Prize (1986), his major published works include *Piano Concertino, Two Movements for Strings* and *Overture for Band, from the Southern Island* (Boosey & Hawkes, New York), *Dialogue for Two Flutes* (Southern Music Company), and *Piano Concerto Fiesta* (Ongaku-no-tomo, Tokyo). Among the books he has published are: *A Music Guide for Parents* (Bungei-Shunju, Japan), *Music Scenes* (Asahi Shinbun, Japan), and *You and Life and Music* (NHK Press).